In Search of
Frog's Legs

In Search of
Frog's Legs

KEN BLACKWELL

© Ken Blackwell, 2025

Published by Ken Blackwell

All rights reserved. No part of this book may be reproduced, adapted, stored in a retrieval system or transmitted by any means, electronic, mechanical, photocopying, or otherwise without the prior written permission of the author.

The rights of Ken Blackwell to be identified as the author of this work have been asserted in accordance with the Copyright, Designs and Patents Act 1988.

A CIP catalogue record for this book is available from the British Library.

ISBN 978-1-5262-1032-6

Manufacturer: York Publishing Services Ltd
64 Hallfield Road, Layerthorpe, York YO31 7ZQ
Tel: 01904 431213 | enquiries@yps-publishing.co.uk
Website: www.yps-publishing.co.uk

Represented by: Authorised Rep Compliance Ltd.
Ground Floor, 71 Lower Baggot Street, Dublin D02 P593, Ireland
www.arccompliance.com

Contents

Chapter One	1
Chapter Two	5
Chapter Three	6
Chapter Four	10
Chapter Five	17
Chapter Six	21
Chapter Seven	23
Chapter Eight	27
Chapter Nine	32
Chapter Ten	34
Chapter Eleven	39
Chapter Twelve	42
Chapter Thirteen	49
Chapter Fourteen	53
Chapter Fifteen	57
Chapter Sixteen	59
Chapter Seventeen	64
Chapter Eighteen	68
Chapter Nineteen	70
Chapter Twenty	72
Chapter Twenty One	75
Chapter Twenty Two	82
Chapter Twenty Three	88

CHAPTER ONE

Off we go …

Rounding a corner on a very minor road, high in the foothills of the French Pyrenees we saw across the sunlit wooded valley a village resting on the opposite hillside. Here in the lonely peace of the mountains we stopped to take in the view, and to dwell on it and to capture it with our camera.

Below us a rocky sparkling ravine with a splashing, noisy waterfall.

The scent of wild flowers warmed by the morning sunshine wafted up.

The village we had found was called Corsavy.

From a distance the impression was the whole village was sliding down the ravine, with houses having been built at all levels. Just the one road passed through the tumbling village. It looked like a place for us to stop and gather, if possible, any old recipes to go in our French rural recipe book. Any chance? … let's see

We drove into the village and looked along the main street, empty except for the only apparent 'inhabitant' an old man relaxing in the afternoon sun outside his cottage in the shade of an old torn awning.

He was seated on a rough carved wooden chair.

We stopped and parked and approached cautiously.

He was indeed an old man his lined face ageing as we got closer.

His bright eyes obviously delighted that someone was stopping to speak to him. He wore not a beret but an old stained trilby, a denim jacket and dark trousers (stained in places) all equally as old.

I asked him in my very best French if he could look at the questionnaire to see if he could help us?"

Ken BLACKWELL, App.28, Residence-du-Port, rue du Lt. Panis, 34350 VALRAS-PLAGE

Je prépare un livre réservé aux touristes anglais qui souhaitent visiter la région. Je vous serais reconnaissant de m'aider dans mes recherches en répondant à ce questionnaire:

1) Pourriez-vous me donner une recette typique de cette region (les ingrédients, le temps de préparation et cuisson et la recette)?

2) Connaissez-vous une anecdote ou une blague qui pourrait figurer dnas ce livre?

3) Citez un lieu qui pourrait intéresser un touriste anglais qui visite la région? (plus particulièrement un site non conseillé par les offices de tourisme)

S'il vous plait, répondez au verso, ou sur une feuille supplémentaire et retournez ce questionnaire dans l'enveloppe timbrée ci-jointe dès que possible.

Si vous souhaitez être cité(e) dans ce livre, précisez votre nom et adresse ci-dessous.

Vous êtes la seule personne de votre village qui possédiez ce questionnaire. Si d'autres personnes souhaitent se joindre à vous pour le remplir, elles seraient les bienvenues, car j'aimerais recueillir le plus d'information possible. Vous pouvez faire appel à votre famille et vos amis.

JE VOUS REMERCIE POUR VOTRE COLLABORATION.

The questionnaire was in perfect French, having been constructed, and examined, then fine-tuned by our neighbour's 14 year old daughter Florence. The questions we had asked Florence to ask were 'Could we please have a family favourite Recipe, a Grandad 'joke' and any local Anecdotes?'

He took the questionnaire and looked at it for some time, his head moving back and forth across the page, smiling from time to time. I looked up and down the dappled street, piles of wood stacked neatly outside the houses. Late August but already well prepared for winter. I wondered what it would be like to live in such a beautiful yet remote place. The road, if it snowed was so narrow it would be blocked in no time. Just how long would this village be cut off.

In the summer months there would be visitors and maybe there were second home owners and tourists passing through.

We only saw two Signs – 'Fromage pur Brebit' and 'Welcome Gites de France'.

I looked at the old gentleman, he was still carefully studying the questionnaire – I decided to suggest to him in my imperfect French that we could come back later, or, maybe his wife would help? I tentatively held out my hand to take back the questionnaire when he suddenly looked up and handed it to me. "I can read only some words Monsieur, but not too many".

I then realized he was unable to read. I thanked him heartily for the time he had given me and we shook hands firmly and with dignity. As we turned to leave he said "If Monsieur would like to leave his paper I will ask my daughter to read it to me".

We left the questionnaire with him along with the stamped addressed reply envelope. He stood and waved to us as we drove off. I watched him in the car mirror and as we drove out of the village he sat back down on his chair holding the questionnaire and peering at it closely once more.

Later his daughter posted it to us, it arrived, saying "this is what my father asked me to tell you, it's this …"

> Our grandfather used to tell us – that he had lost the chance of a lifetime to get rich.
>
> "When I was 20 I went to the fair' he recalled – La Foire aux Nefles at Sevres.

This translates roughly as the 'Sod-all Fair' and Sevres is a village not far from Lagrasse.

At this Fair they were selling ten litre measures of 'sod all' for one old FRANC and the same measure in gold coins for 5 FRANCS. Having only one FRANC in my pocket I bought the measure of 'nothing' and I returned home that day as poor as I am today".

editor's note ('no I don't get it either')

Also, I remember him saying he used to travel down the valley on his old rusty bike to help with the grape harvest (the vendange). And this is the grape harvest lunch his Mother would prepare and which he would take with him to the vineyard wrapped in an old tea cloth'.

DEJEUNER DE VENDANGE

Rub some garlic onto a slice of bread which had been doused in local olive oil.

Eat with black grapes and a glass of Cinsaut, Terret, Aramon de Coreau.

Or

Grape harvester's sour herring.

Cut some sour herring into small pieces along with an onion doused with local olive oil. Eat with bread covered in olive oil so as to soften the taste.

Cinsaut, Terret or Aramon de Coteau grapes.

CHAPTER TWO

Dogs on holiday – cat extra

French holidaymakers arrive at this resort (Valras Plage) by plane at the local airport from Paris. My sister-in-law, coming to visit us from Grassington in the Yorkshire Dales, where dogs are dogs and expected to work for their living) and flying from Manchester via Paris, told us that on the internal flights, the plane was like a travelling 'Crufts'.

There were small doggies of all descriptions on passengers laps. She said she felt fortunate the flights was too short to warrant a meal, otherwise she had visions of bowls of 'Pedigree Chum' being handed round. She told us that even on the carousel, on arrival, there were as many dogs (the larger ones) coming round in cages as there was suitcases.

So if you come here for a holiday … watch your step!

CHAPTER THREE

Frogs Legs and Snails

Two things to look out for on the menu here, and you may wish to avoid, are 'escargots' (snails) and 'cuise de grenouille', (frog's legs).

It's only the back legs of the frog that are eaten as a delicacy but, of course this raises the question as to just who it was who discovered it was only the 'back' legs that were tasty.

Whoever it was, did he, for example come home one day with a frog and say to his wife, "Here dear, just pop this in the frying pan will you I'm going to eat it", and then sat down and ate it all, which he must have done, in order to be able to declare "The back legs are OK, but forget the rest! "

And snails? Now just who was it who first picked up a snail and ate it? I suspect this same chap once more, and, furthermore, because it is recommended that snails are left to clean themselves, by hanging them in a wire basket for up to three weeks, before eating, who was it? who tried them after Day 1, Day 2, Day 3 … and so on to be able to declare, after 21 days of eating them, "Nope, it takes three weeks before they are really fit to eat!"

Whoever he was, he deserves rightful recognition.

BON APPETIT

And that reminds me of another thing you may wish to avoid. Some years ago, while on holiday with our friends, Pete and June we visited a restaurant in the Auvergne region of France and, as no one except me knew any French I translated the menu.

June asked what 'cervelle d'agneau' was and I translated this as 'lamb chop'. I should have asked the waiter to explain, he did speak some English, but, when you're showing off you don't like to.

The other three of us got our different orders, but June was served a white plate on which appeared to be a large dollop of cold rice pudding … it was brains!

We decided the best policy was to wrap it up in two paper napkins from the table, and June put it in her handbag to dispose of later. I couldn't apologise enough but just then the waiter came back to our table and said, in the fashion of waiters "Is everything to your satisfaction?"

We three had only just started and mumbled. "Fine thank you".

He then looked in astonishment at June's completely empty plate.

She smiled at him sweetly and said "Delicious".

Whilst many foreigners are inclined to believe that 'frog's legs' form a good part of the French diet, along with 'snails', well, we've haven't often seen them on menus or at the supermarket only rarely.

I have kept a note of the 'French' names -'Cuisse de Grenouille' (leg/thigh noun feminine frog cuisse = thigh and 'escargots' (noun masculin Snails) so we can all look out for them and thus avoid them? but nay you may wish to try them?

We'll put any 'menus' (masc plural) we find for you, in this book before the last page!

La Famille en Or'.

On TV here in France is a programme called 'La Famille en Or', you know the one – 'Family Fortunes' it's where they ask 100 people various questions and competing family groups have to guess which is the most correct and popular answer.

One question on the programme last night was "What is the most common way of hurting oneself?

The most common, of course, was hitting one's thumb with a hammer when hitting in a nail!

However the THIRD most common way, in France according to this programme to hurt oneself was whilst opening …

OYSTERS!

Now I wonder where that would rank in England?

Our idea was developing. My wife and I would travel the rural routes of Southern France asking local people if they had old recipes and could we be allowed to copy them to help us put together a book!

We'd seek out old, nearly forgotten recipes, and ask for anecdotes, family tales etc from this rural population and jokes? No doubt they will have a selection for us.

And of course all the while we'd be enjoying ourselves and getting to understand the French way of life and culture and maybe, although we'd never done it before – produce a book!

Is there anyone reading this book? Have we done it …?

CHAPTER FOUR

Our Next Outing

In our quest for rural recipes, we set off! 'Up' into the foothills of the high Pyrenees – starting from sea-level and heading for the mountains and the town of Prades. … there was a clear dazzling light this sunny morning.

We had a glorious view driving up the mountainside road, looking down over fields full of blue flowers, above us were mountain tops and streams cascaded out onto the road.

These streams were then directed by 'culverts' – through tunnels under the road, thus to avoid the road getting washed away. They found their freedom again on the other side where they gushed out with quite a force and tumbling on created a 'mist' shimmering with all the colours of Monet, et Manet.

On the road and coming downhill at great speed towards us, were groups of cyclists, all of whom looked over 60. plus! They were wearing brightly coloured jerseys adorned with Company advertising. These 'elderly' seemed pretty fit with their logos for 'Pastis Ricard', 'Courvoisier Cognac' and 'Gauloise' cigarettes. They streamed passed us with a wave and off down into the valley below.

We followed the signpost into the village of Fillols – now this is rural, a village of quaint houses with various pastel shades with shutters bathing in the soft sunshine. In the village centre was a small 'square' overlooked by the Town Hall, the 'Mairie' Honey coloured walls and wrought-iron balconies. Everywhere dripping with red geraniums to fully compose a picture.

Clearing tables outside the cafe, we met an elderly lady dressed all in black.

We offered her our questionnaire and explained that it had been prepared with the aid of our neighbour's 14 year old French daughter FLORENCE, who had overseen the lay-out and the typing of the form and herself had run off for us exactly 100 photocopies to be distributed!

We explained to the old lady that was why the form was in 'perfect' French as why we ourselves were not fluent, not by a long chalk sorry.

She understood and looking at both sides made the point of explaining to us that was why the form was in English one side, and French on the other.

She said it was all 'Formidable'.

Furthermore, she added it was 'tres interessant'.

We showed her the stamped addressed reply-envelope so that 'when she had time' she could perhaps write for us a recipe!

She said that she would be pleased to help, but it was her daughter who owned the café and we must speak with her first. We followed our lady indoors, being carefully observed from the bar by four seated male villagers who were studying old newspapers and drinking their morning's pastis.

We explained ourselves to her daughter, the imposing matron standing behind the bar cleaning glasses.

'Madame Escape', she introduced herself – being the sole owner since the sad demise of her husband, of the "Cafe de L'Union" and, "Oui", after glancing further at the questionnaire she declared she would be pleased to help.

"She could give us some country recipes if we wished to have them, and she said she had undoubtedly some good yarns which her bar clients had told her over the years!

After a few days the recipes arrived all squashed into our envelope and tied around with tape – including a considerable assortment of very grubby 'pastis-stained' pieces of paper. All written in heavy pencil and taking considerable deciphering, but, they were the start we needed, and 'fitted the bill as promised'

These are Madam Escape's recipes.

SAUTE DE VEAU CHASSEUR
(VEAL WITH TOMATOES AND MUSHROOMS)

750g pie veal	25g flour
25g butter	125ml white wine
1 tbsp olive oil	250ml stock
4 shallots	salt and pepper
1 clove garlic	150g button mushrooms
4 tomatoes	25 black olives

Cut the meat into cubes, heat the butter and oil in a pan and fry the shallots, garlic and meat together for about 10 minutes. Skin the tomatoes, cut into quarters and remove pips. Add to the pan and cook.

Season with salt and pepper, cover pan and simmer gently for 30 minutes.

Fifteen minutes before the end of cooking add the mushrooms and olives.

Serves 4

STUFFED TOMATOES

large firm ripe tomatoes
1 cup dry white breadcrumbs, not too fine.
1/3 to ½ cup of olive oil
½ cup finely chopped fresh parsley
1 tablespoon finely cut fresh basil or 2 tablespoon dry basil.
1 large garlic, finely chopped.
Salt & freshly ground black pepper.

Cut tomatoes in half-crosswise. With a finger or teaspoon scoop out the seeds. Sprinkle the inside of tomatoes with salt and turn them upside-down to drain on paper towel. Preheat oven to 375 degrees.

In a large mixing bowl, stir together the breadcrumbs, parsley, basil, garlic, 1 teaspoon salt and a few grindings of pepper. Add enough olive oil to moisten the stuffing but still leave it crumbly.

Fill each tomato half with about 2 tablespoons of the mixture, patting it in and letting it mound up in the middle. Arrange tomato halves in lightly oiled shallow dish, not too close. Sprinkle a few drops of oil over each half. Bake in the upper third of the oven for 20 to 30 minutes, or until the tomatoes are tender but not limp.

With a wide spatula, transfer the tomatoes to a heated plate and serve them hot or chill the tomatoes and serve them cold, sprinkled with chopped parsley.

Please note all the recipes in this book are as received by us, translated by us and Florence, and of course care must be taken to ensure that your ingredients throughout are fresh and wholesome.

Here are four stories from the bar of the Cafe de L'Union

1. The old goat of Mere Lemiche was ill. She took him to the veterinaire who examined him and declared:–

    "He is quite ill, your goat, you must keep him warm".

    "In that case I'm going to put it in my bed"

    "What on earth are you thinking of Mere Lemiche? said the vet. "What about the smell?" "Oh, I'm sure he'll get used to it", she replied.

2. A peasant from the countryside around Fillols, was walking down the village street wearing a smart cravat with a very large diamond pin. His friend stopped him and enquired "that diamond it's magnificent have you won the lottery?

    "Oh no was the reply but you remember my neighbour Andre, that bachelor? Well just before he died he said he wanted me to spend his entire fortune on a commemorative stone! – so this is it'

3. A little pig was sitting in the corner of the farmyard. A traveller noticed it had two wooden legs and exclaimed to the farmer – "It's incredible, you loving your animal to such a degree to provide him with wooden legs".

    "Ah yes, think of it, we love him so much we're only eating him little by little.

4. Next Bernard from Fillols, a peasant, was invited as a guest to the Chateau.

He asked a more knowledgeable friend – "when I'm there if I want to go to the WC, what do I say to the lady of the house?"

It's a simple matter of saying, replied his friend, "could you please tell me where I could wash my hands".

On arrival the next day, at the chateau the lady of the house welcomed him and said, "Ah Bernard, would you like to wash your hands?"

"No thank you Madam" he replied, "I've just washed them in your driveway".

Joke from the Café de L'Union (Prades/Fillols)

CHAPTER FIVE

Pretty Rural

Now for somewhere even higher in the Pyrenees, the D4C or the D4E to Talau. It was the best of days, it was the worst of narrow roads. It was a time to go forward, it was time to be sensible and turn back. It was in short the road to Talau.

A road that clung to the mountainside and twisted and turned, then turned and getting narrower twisted again.

A road, from humble beginnings down in a housing estate in the town of Olette had laboured up and up to become one of the highest roads in the land!

It was the dickens of a road.

We had a choice, one of two. The D4E, which according to our map became a dotted line! or the D4C, which ceased on the map at a shape like an 'arrowhead' and then recommence, a short while after, from a further 'arrowhead'.

What on earth did it mean? Here we were high up in the Pyrenees – hadn't seen a soul for miles.

We chose the D4E and on turning the first corner stopped. A large barbeque had been put together in the middle of the road! A black metal grill over a lively wood burning pan on which large steaks were sizzling, being turned, and cooked.

 We stopped the car and got out there was no way to pass. There we met four huntsmen who had caught a wild boar (sanglier) that very morning.

We sought confirmation we were on the right road which they confirmed and asked, "Would Monsieur and Madame like to try a sanglier steak?"

"Bien-sur" we would.

They explained they had built the barbeque on the road as of course the vegetation on the mountainside was very dry because of the 'chaleur,' and there was grave risk of fire, and besides, "no one ever comes along this road".

We were given a knife and fork, a plate with a large sizzling steak, and of course large chunks of bread.

A few glasses of local red wine later we were asked, "and the 'sanglier' caught in England is it as good?"

"Oh no" we said, "but it was passable".

We produced our enquiry form and explained our task. They discussed the request at great length and asked would we like from them their recipe for Civet de Sanglier.? (wild boar stew) to try a 'comparison' with the English wild boar when we got back home".

Yes please … and here it is!"

'LE VOICI'

For 4 persons

Take 1 kilo of sanglier, 1 litre of Fitou, 2 onions, 6 cloves of garlic, bouquet garni, salt, pepper, 100g flour.

Macerate the sanglier cut into small pieces, add wine, bouquet garni and leave overnight.

The next day strain the liquid, keeping the juices, and place in a casserole with a little olive oil, salt and pepper to taste. Then flambe the dish with a large glass of Armanac, pour back the wine juices and cook for 3 to 4 hours.

Thicken with flour and serve.

CIVET de SANGLIER

POUR 4 pers

1 kg Sanglier - 1 Ltrs de Fitou - 2 oignons - 6 Ails.
Bouquets garnis - Sel-poivre - 150 g farine -

- Faire macerer le Sanglier coupé en morceaux dans le vin avec le Bouquet garni pendant 1 nuit.

- Le lendemain, mettre le sanglier dans 1 cocotte avec un peu d'huiles, le faire bien roussir, ajouter l'ail et oignons hachés, sel, poivre, flambé avec un jus d'armagnac, ensuite mettre le vin et faire mijoter 3/4 heures.

- Avant de servir, prendre la farine et faire une liaison.

Situé sur la route des châteaux cathares entre CUCUGNAN et DUILHAC le lac vous offre toutes les joies pour l'été.

CHAPTER SIX

Miss Valras Plage

On returning from the hills we ate a very light supper, showered and changed for an evening's stroll along the sea front.

At the open-air theatre was the 'Miss Valras' competiton. We sat and watched along with all the many other theatre-goers.

One young lady Stephanie in her 'evening dress' (which really consisted of no more than the shortest of mini-skirts and a T shirt which proclaimed 'PAS PARFAIT MAIS PRESQUE' she was questioned in the usual manner by the compere.

"If you could take out for an evening's candle-lit dinner for two any man in the whole world, who would that be?"

"Jean-Pierre from the Hotel Moderne", she replied. And when the compere asked where Jean-Pierrre was, she pointed to the back of the audience.

"Il est la", whereupon the young man operating the spotlights sprung into action and picked out Jean-Pierre in the audience. The lights dimmed and two spotlights narrowed into two small circles: one on the face of Stephanie (on the stage) and one on the face of Jean-Pierre (at the back of the audience) the rest in darkness.

"Now Stephanie" said the compere "do you have a message for Jean-Pierre?"

"Oui" she whispered into the microphone, "je t'aime."

"Ahhh!" sighed the audience.

"And how long have you known Jean-Pierre?" asked the compere – "three days" was the reply!

Then things got rather interesting -Stephanie in the manner of beauty queens went backstage to change into her bathing costume for the finale.

Virginie was next and was asked all the usual questions of a prospective beauty Queen.

She also was asked "If you could take out for an evening 'candle-lit' – 'dinner for two', any man in the whole world who would it be?"

"Jean-Pierre from the Hotel Moderne" she replied.

At that the spotlight man sprang into action to pin-point Jeane-Pierre once more at the back, but … he was gone.

The audience of course loved it but poor innocent Virginie had no idea what all the laughter was about and neither did poor Stephanie when she came back later in her bikini.

The whole evening ended in uproar when the 'compere' with all the contestants lined up on the stage, mixed up the winner with the runner up (neither of our two young ladies by the way) by making the wrong announcement! – the judges chosen beforehand from various sections of the audience all rushed up the steps onto the stage to correct him – He had to take the sash and flowers from one girl and give them to another. Of course the loser then burst into tears with her family and supporters shouting from the audience.

A really entertaining evening we also joined in the shouts of protest and thoroughly enjoyed ourselves.

CHAPTER SEVEN

The Corrieu family

La Llagonne, a village of 240 souls, backing onto the Capcir plateau at an altitude of 168m. is known throughout Europe as a 'hang – gliding' and Nordic Ski centre.

In fact thanks to the purity of the air and the thermals created in La Llagonne's Mediterranean sky, those great birds of wood and cloth, reach extraordinary heights.

When in 1965, a Monsieur Pic beat the world altitude record for one of these machines at 10,000m he was approaching par with the jumbos!

In winter a considerable number of cross-country skiers set out from this picturesque village to follow the marked ski routes, trekking through pine forests to reach the wild open spaces. Our stop in this region was at the Hotel Corrieu where we met family Corrieu.

They told us that their hotel was built over a century ago and was at that time, a coaching house where coaches stopped overnight and replenished. Travellers crossing the plateau of Capcir broke their journeys here, before continuing down to the Cerdagne plain.

The remains of the very old timbered stables are still visible today.

After the war this hotel underwent extensive refurbishment and now offers guests all mod cons and an unbeaten warmth of hospitality.

"This being a characteristic of four generations of the Corrieu family".

So if you want to try this hospitality the address is:-

Hotel Corrieu – 66210 La Llagonne
tel.no. 68.04.22.04

This is a local recipe kindly given to us by the hotel's chef – M. Maurice Corrieu.

LOUILLADE

Louillade is a typical Capcir dish and which is especially welcome during the winter evenings.

- 1 cabbage (one which has tasted it's first frost)
- Good Capcir potatoes
- 5 carrots, 3 leeks, 1 stick of celery and 3 turnips.
- 1 pig's trotter and some pig's offle.(sic)
- 1 knuckle of veal
- 1 shin of beef
- 2 black puddings

After having scalded the pieces of pork, cook them for an hour. Then add the veal and beef and continue cooking for 2 ½ hours.

Next add the vegetables, Cut into 2cm. long pieces, flour).

The cooking should be done throughout on a low heat, preferably in an 'ouille' so as to ensure a consistent heat and a very tasty stew.

The 'ouille' is a cast iron pot which is hung over the chimney fire.

And another recipe

LE FREGINAT (FRICASSEE OF PORK)

Le Freginat for 5-6 people

1 kilo of pork back-bone,
1 kilo of pork neck with sweetbreads
4 or 5 kidneys
a piece of spleen

Cut all into small pieces – about 2 cm pieces.

Place in pot – add a soup spoonful of pig fat and 3 to 4 spoonfuls of olive oil.

Cook slowly without browning the meat.

Meanwhile finely chop two gloves of garlic and a handful of parsley.

Black tomato puree should be home made and salty enough. No more salt is therefore needed in the recipe.

Dilute this with a small bowlful of white wine vinegar.

Once diluted pour over meat and cover meat with boiling water.

Leave to cook for an hour and half.

For even better results prepare the meat the day before the sauce.

This Freginat is eaten with haricot or kidney beans and to be eaten with a lump of bread and slices of milla – a porridge of cooked white maize.

This is a favourite traditional family dish, one made when one kills a pig.

DESERT

Take hard almond nut shells – wash the broken almond shells, after having removed the almonds. In a pan add 1/3 of the shells to 2/3 water.

Boil and eat when soft, with romarin honey or even sugar. Also excellent with milk.

And the Corrieu family joke!

A car was stopped by the gendarmes for speeding on the Route Nationale between St. Chinian and Beziers.

"Bonjour monsieur – at what speed were you travelling"

"Oh at 90 kms, no more"

"You think so, eh? We registered more than that, would you please blow into this bag for the alcool test"

The driver blew and was registered as 'positif'

"But that can't be possible, Monsieur le Gendarme, I've only drunk water, ask my wife, we've spent the whole day together"

"In that case perhaps Madame would care to blow into the bag?"

She did and was also registered 'positif'

"This can't be" said the driver, "your equipment must be faulty, I'll tell you what try the little one, he's only drunk milk"

They roused the baby on the back seat and he blew into the bag. again positif.

The two gendarmes looked at each other in amazement, apologised profusely and they waved the car on it's way.

After a few kilometers, as the baby dozed off again the husband turned to his wife and "There you are, I told you that baby would sleep better with some brandy in his milk"

CHAPTER EIGHT

Conilhac ... the place of rabbits

It was one of those hot Mediterranean afternoons, lunch had been partaken of, so with little further to do for the moment the townsfolk, those well passed retirement age would bring outside their front doors, a straight backed chair to sit.

Maybe to dream in the shade and just to watch as the world rolls by.

Workmen of all varieties dash by in little citroyen vans, men and women return to the vineyards – as the VENDANGE had begun.

Children trudged back to their afternoon's classes, and tourists parked their cars in the hot sun of the municipal parking area.

Their plans being to take a stroll around the village and maybe pause in some shaded pavement café.

Getting into the shade wherever possible.

Afternoon life of this town of Conilac, department of Languedoc/Rousillon.

We also pulled into the municipal parking area. A number of local people, old ladies dressed all in black most of the men wearing berets. Just the sort of established local folk we were looking to complete our recipe plus survey.

They were gathering as a boules tournament was about to begin. I got out of the car and approached them.

Before I had time to tell them about our questionaire, our 'raison d'etre' – they had seen the 'G.B'. Sticker.

They spoke almost as one pleased to see us, "Ah, Anglais? et La Reine? Elle va bien?"

"Yes" I replied, as far as I am aware Her Majesty was quite well, but unfortunately, as they were probably aware (or the French or English Press hadn't been doing its usual job) there had been some difficult times for her nearest and dearest "Ah yes, and Lady Dee? Elle est si belle".

"Oui" we all agreed on that.

They asked as she was now 'available' would I personally be making her acquaintance?

I sighed. I motioned towards my wife who was still in the car and tapped my wedding ring with a sigh and a newly acquired French 'shrug'

"Ahh", they understood.

As there were now eight potential helpers gathered round I explained, "Could he, with the help of all those 'gathered here' fill in my questionaire?"

He read it out carefully and slowly and then said that he personally would undertake to send me all the information I needed.

I thanked him. He was, he said and here he touched his beret with his forefinger and thumb, "Andre Saly of Place De l'Horloge, Conilhac".

I thanked him again. "Pas de probleme Monsieur", he replied.

"Dites Bonjour a la Reine de moi".

If you ever visit Conilhac do lookout for Andre Saly. You will find him wearing a black beret, playing boules alongside the municipal parking area.

Tell him Her Majesty thanks him and also says 'Bonjour'.

Andre Saly of Conilhac, Corbiers writes:

> Conilhac, small village of Corbiers in L'Aude, is situated at the side of the Route National 113, midway between Carcassonne and Narbonne, a village which possess a large expanse of vines which produce a 'vin rouge' of the highest quality.
>
> The wine growers are proud of their wine and sell it wholesale in bulk or in bottles at the Cave Cooperative or at the storehouse of the individual producers.
>
> Their love of wine does not diminish their love for the hunt or tracking in the garrigue, where the lapin lives and prospers in abundance, nourishing himself on the wild plants au perfum which give it its particular flavour.
>
> The cooks take great care in preparing the succulent 'civets' (rabbit stews) and jealously guard the secret recipes.
>
> For my own part it will give me great pleasure to release my own secret recipe to you.
>
> First of all though, you must note the very old origins of the name of our village.
>
> Conilhac, comes from the 'Counil' – (lapin) and 'hac' (place – lieu) the place of the rabbits.

We now come to the making of our 'civet'

Take a rabbit killed in our garrigue. Place some of the blood in a container with a few drops of vinegar. Cut the rabbit into 12 pieces, peel an onion and two shallots and some cloves of garlic.

Brown the pieces of rabbit and flambe them with some FINE brandy of the Languedoc.

Brown onions along with the the garlic.

Season with salt and pepper to taste and throw in thyme and a bay-leaf.

Throw in 75cl of vin rouge de Corbier (from Conilhac de peference) add a handful of lardons and porc roussis (brown pieces of pork).

Leave to cook on a low heat for about an hour.

Restillier la sauce s'il y a lieu before serving by making a mixture of the blood and chopped liver and 2 grains of garlic.

A good Corbiers Rouge is recommended with this dish and as Monsieur Saly writes as he ends his recipe:-

"BON APPETIT"

After thinking over how Andre Saly had expressed genuine concern regarding the Royal Family, and he clearly was most concerned, I thought why not? It would be a pleasant surprise for him.

So a letter was despatched to Buckingham Palace asking if it would be possible, in view of the kind thoughts he expressed in a small village in the south of France to write a letter of thanks? I'm sure you'll know full well that a kind reply was received from Her Majesty as follows.

K. Blackwell Esq

BUCKINGHAM PALACE

Dear Mr. Blackwell

I write to thank you for your letter which I had the honour of laying before The Queen.

Her Majesty thought it was kind of you to write of your experiences in France while researching for your recipe book.

Although it is not possible to send a letter direct to Monsieur Saly owing to the enormous amount of mail received each day, perhaps you would let him know that The Queen was touched to learn of his concern and I am to thank him also for his greetings.

Yours sincerely,

Richenda Elton

Lady – in – Waiting.

I'm pleased to tell you that a photocopy of the above letter was posted on to Monsieur Saly the very next day.

CHAPTER NINE

Benny Hill

Benny Hill is very popular here in France. Thames T.V. have compiled a foreign language version of the shows.

Occasionally where a sketch does have dialogue it is 'dubbed' into French. We have a neighbour who claims he does the French version of the 'voice-over' for these TV shows, Jean-Michel – He greeted me in the lift when we were both leaving the 'Residence du Port' at the same time.

He was keen to ask what I thought of his version of last night's show? and he mimed scantily attired young ladies and gently waving palm trees with coconuts, and then with great gusto high winds and again with scantily attired young ladies and again even more coconuts. In fact our neighbour 'Jean-Michel' is quite a mime artist.

We had both parked our cars at the beachside car park. This morning we happened to be parked alongside each other – us with plans to set off to some rural villages to search out recipes.

Both cars were totally covered in sand, and Jean-Michel proceeded to mime riding a horse, but indicated it had a large lump in front of the rider, and a large lump behind a camel!

He mimed gently waving palm trees and then with great gusto, a howling wind and the blowing of a great sandstorm.

He pointed across the Mediterranean to the source of this gargantuan storm – the deserts of North Africa. Further gestures indicated powerful air currents carrying the sand vertically, up from the desert and high into the atmosphere, across the sea and, eh voila! down onto our cars.

"Ah, I said, "I understand" as he got into his Renault 12 and drove off, obviously pleased with this enlightenment of his English friends.

Why, however, he didn't think it had just blown off the beach, which was only 100 yards away, I don't know.

We drove off grains of Sahara sand blowing away behind us.

CHAPTER TEN

The Car Wash

We arrived in the rural village of Vingrau in glorious sunshine at lunchtime. Of course there was no-one out of doors in that heat except one man with a hose-pipe. He was jet-washing over 40, large plastic containers. They were to be left till after lunch and then placed on trailers behind small tractors and be carried back to the vineyards, there to be filled with more ripened grapes.

This process of filling the containers and, bringing back to the village 'co-operative'- emptying, taking back to the vineyard and so on, would continue until late evening.

Chalked on is the name of the variety of grape to be tipped into that particular hopper.

Shown today:

Blanc

Cepages Rouge Carignan

Cepages Rouge

Syrah

Alicote Merlot2,

Selection Terroirer

lot3-4 Autres Cepages

autres 3-4

Blanc

Cepages Rouge Carignan

Cepages Rouge

Syrah

Alicote Merlot2,

Selection Terroirer

lot3-4 Autres Cepages

He studied our car for a moment, whilst playing the hose on the plastic containers. We explained our plan to gather recipes.

I showed him our questionnaire' and the reply-paid envelope.

He looked at me, peered into the car to look at my wife, looked more closely at the still sand-stained car bodywork and said that yes he would be pleased to give us a recipe but first he must wash our car!

He motioned to my wife to wind up her window and there at the side of Rue Paul Riquet, Vingrau my Rover regained it's metallic blue colour all thanks to the kindness of Monsieur Ferrer and his hosepipe.

We left him with the questionnaire and our grateful thanks.

A few days later we received this recipe from Madame Ferrer at the Cave Co-operative.

HARICOT DE MOUTON

(HARICOT BEANS AND LAMB – A GOOD ECONOMICAL COUNTRY DISH)

375g (12oz) haricot beans
salt
25g (1oz) butter
2 large onions
2 cloves garlic crushed
750g (1½ lbs) lean stewing lamb or mutton
400ml (¾ pint stock)
1 bouquet garni
1 sprig thyme
freshly milled black pepper

Soak the beans overnight in cold water.

Drain, cover with fresh cold water and a little salt and bring to boil.

Cover and simmer gently for 30 minutes.

Melt butter in a large pan, add the onions and garlic and fry for 5 minutes.

Chop the lamb into small cubes and add to the onions and fry for another 5 – 10 minutes.

Pour the stock over the meat, add the bouquet garni, thyme, pepper and drained beans.

Cover the pan and simmer gently for 2 ½ hours.

Remove the bouguet garni before serving.

Serves 4.

Oh yes and M. Ferrrer's joke

A man went to his barbers and while his hair was being cut discussed his forthcoming holiday.

"My wife and I are flying 'Air France' to Rome, staying in the Hotel des Ducs, touring the city and having an audience with the Pope".

The barber clipping away said "You've chosen the worst airline company, the Hotel des Ducs is dreadful.

Rome is awful at this time of year and there will be thousands of people there to see the Pope".

On his next visit a month later, he was asked by the barber "and your holiday?"

"Perfect" he replied, "flight super, hotel superb and Rome was so beautiful and not only that we had a private audience with the Pope."

"No kidding" said the barber.

"Yes" said the customer, "and he gave me his personal blessing. The only thing was when he placed his hands on my head he said, "Who on earth cut your hair? Take my advice and change your barber!

3) A 15 Kms de Narbonne ce trouve un petit Hameau qui s'APPELLE LE SOMAIL.
. Il est traversé par le canal du Midi.
C'est un petit village très beau et beaucoup touristique depuis la construction de son Domaine Hôtelier en pleine campagne.
Il y a aussi son Musée de la Chapellerie, un musée de POTERIE, de peinture.

- Melle MICHEL Anne
Avenue de la République
11 120 St Nazaire d'Aude

CHAPTER ELEVEN

TRUE CASSOULET

Here is the recipe from the equivalent of a District Nurse from the town of Capendu.

It is, we are assured the correct method of preparation with the correct ingredients.

The recipes for this particular dish vary considerably all over the region.

The town of Castelnaudary, however, lays claim to the true recipe using the authentic ingredients, and to support their claim they have created a 'Brotherhood of Master Cassoulet Chefs' called the 'Grande Confrerie du Cassoulet de Castelnaudary'.

As Capendu is some distance from Castelnaudary, our district nurse could be open to challenge.

Here it is …

for 8 persons – cooking time 3 hours

Ingredients
1 shoulder of mutton, boned and cut into pieces
300gr of fresh blade of pork
150gr belly pork
300gr of saucisse de Toulouse
1 saucisson a l'ail de 300gr
2 onions
1 litre of white haricot beans
1 tete d'ail

500g. Tomatoes
50g. of lard
Thyme, bay leaves and breadcrumbs
salt and pepper

Soak the haricot beans for several hours in cold water.

Cook beans for ½ hour in salted water then drain.

In a casserole dish place the pieces of mutton with blade of pork and the belly pork.

Add the lard. Cook on high heat until pieces are golden brown, then add beans, chopped garlic, thyme, bay leaves and cloves.

Cover with water, mixing well add salt and pepper.

Allow to cook on a low heat for about 1½ hours, watching from time to time, adding more water if level gets too low.

After 1 hour of cooking add garlic saucisson.

Faites revenir (separately in a knob of lard) the saucisson of Toulouse and then put on one side.

Prepare a puree of tomatoes by chopping them and cooking them with the finely cut onions for about 15 minutes.

Arrange around the casserole which had been cooking, the meat, beans, the saucisson de Toulouse cut into fine slices. Mix all.

Add tomato puree, sprinkle with breadcrumbs and allow to brown in the oven for a few minutes.

Serve in the casserole, piping hot.

Recommended wine – Cahors

Here are the district nurse's jokes.

A peasant went to the Doctors who examined him but found all in order.

As a precaution however, he asked the peasant to bring in a 'sample'.

The peasant returned with a 2 litre bottle, completely full!

The Doctor only needed of course, a small amount but to save the peasant any embarrassment, said nothing and sent the 2 litre bottle to the lab for analysis.

All was in order and he told the peasant accordingly who went home happily to tell his wife "I'm OK you are OK … the kids are OK, so are both Grandma and Grandad and so's the cat.

A peasant telephoned the Doctor.

"How much do you charge per visit to your surgery"

The Doctor replied "200 francs for the first visit, and 100 francs for each of the following visits".

The peasant arrived the next day and went into the consulting room.

Bonjour Doctor, C'est moi encore".

The Doctor examined him and said "Still the same, carry on with the treatment I recommended last time"

The country Doctor was 'truly desole" when he had to announce to his patient "There is nothing I can do for you, you have an heredity desease".

"In that case" the patient replied. "Send your bill to my father!"

CHAPTER TWELVE

There are still, in certain parts of France, bullfighting arenas, where Spanish-style bullfighting takes place. Bulls are reared just for the sport and are killed by highly, colourfully dressed 'Matadors'. However only after the Bull has been 'weakened'.

This is done by firstly 'Peones' who tease and tire the bull by angering it, encouraging it to run back and forth by waving their arms in front.

The Peones then retire safely behind protective wooden barriers. The bull is then weakened further by 'Picadors' who sit on horses clad in protective chain-mail and, wearing 'blinkers' so the horses are not frightened by the sight of the bull. They lance and pierce the flesh.

The lances remain in the bull's side. The lances with coloured favours pierce the skin and muscles all along the bulls neck and back.

Next the 'Banderillos' take over. They dash towards the disorientated bull, jumping and planting steel spikes with a ribbon into the neck and back.

Finally the 'Matador' with red cape in hand and spurred on by the cheers of the crowd delivers the coup de grace, a final blow of mercy as the dictionary describes it. They plunge a sword between the bull's shoulder blades and into its heart.

In Beziers there are bullfights.

After a bullfight the carcases are purchased by local butchers.

The meat is then cut and sold in their shops.

Here is a recipe from Madame Montagne of Beziers for bull meat Stew.

Daube de toro — Béziers

Vin conseillé : Vin rosé ou Vin rouge

p/ 4 personnes

- 1 kg. p/ Daube de toro de corrida
- 100 grammes de lardons fumés
- 500 grammes carottes
- 1 litre, et demi de bon vin Rouge 11°
- 2 feuilles de laurier
- 1 branche de thym
- 3 à 4 oignons ou échalottes
- 1 gousse d'ail ou (tête d'ail)

La veille faire macérer la viande avec le vin rouge + carottes coupées en rondelles + thym + laurier + oignons coupés en rondelles) + ail et mettre au réfrigérateur. 24 heures au moins.

Le lendemain - faire revenir la viande dans de l'huile. La saler, la poivrer, et mettre tous les ingrédients qui ont macéré avec la viande (soient: vin rouge - épices - carottes, oignons) et faire cuire au moins 2 heures 30 à petits feux ou à la cocotte-minute 1h30 - la viande doit être bien <u>cuite</u> - si la sauce est trop liquide là délayée avec un peu de maïzena (fécule de maïs) et faire cuire 5 minutes.

Plat excellent accompagné de pâtes ou pommes de terre cuites à la vapeur

DAUBE DE TORRO

For 4 persons – in case you should ever wish to try it.
take
1 Kilo of fresh Corrida bull meat
100 gms of smoked lardons (finely cubed pieces of bacon)
500gm of carrots
1 ½ litres of good vin rouge
2 Bay leafs
1 Sprig of thyme
3 or 4 shallots
1 gousse (clove) of garlic

The evening before the meal, macerate the meat with the red wine and sliced carrots.

Add garlic and leave in fridge for 24 hours at least.

The next day, place in a large casserole dish (La cocotte) the meat and juices, salt and pepper and all ingredients and cook for at least 2 ½ hours on a low heat.

If the sauce is too liquid thicken with a little (rocule de mais) maize flour and cook for a further 5 minutes.

An excellent accompaniment to this dish are (pate de terre) steamed potatoes.

From the Chateau of Lastours

LA BOURRIDE D'ANGUILLES
(A BROTH OF EEL STEW)

La Bourride is a typical Mediterranean dish and a firm favourite with the fishermen that live in the Languedoc/Roussillon region.

The l'anguille (eel) is a very sought after creature for the quality of the flesh is very fine.

This dish can also be made with fish – lotte (burbot)

Recipe is for 6 people

Ingredients
200gms of lard (lard ranee)
3 cloves of garlic
3 eggs
3 piments de cayenne (3 cayenne peppers)
some grains of aniseed
toasted bread
½ litre of olive oil
600gms of eels
400gms of potatoes
2 thin slices of bayonne ham (jambon sec)
salt and pepper

Confectionner une pommade (beat together to make a paste) with the lard ranee and garlic, jambon sec.

Melt the mixture in a casserole on a medium heat. Peel and wash potatoes.

Cut them into slices 3cms thick, add the potatoes to the pomade fundue, (well blended).

Add peppers, grains of aniseed and cover with water.

Scrape the eels with sand to clean the skin, wash thoroughly.

De-head and gut them. Add them to the potatoes and eat with mayonnaise (aioli)

Crush in an earthenware pot the garlic, salt, pepper and three egg yolks.

Slowly mix the mayonnaise with olive oil.

Cut three slices of bread per person – cover each slice with the mayonnaise and grill.

After 20 minutes of cooking the bourride, mix the ailio into the bourride.

Decorate the serving dish with the grilled bread and cover with the bourride.

serve

(pris servis an assiett)- sorry don't know what this means?

The jokes from the chateau

Two ladies were talking on the quayside at the port of Marsielle.

"My husband came home from fishing last night, but he's off again tomorrow."

"You don't see him very often then?", enquired her friend.

"No, only about 40 days each year".

"Oh how awful for you!"

"Well you know 40 days they soon pass!"

The teacher asked Marcel's father to come into school.

"I'm afraid I've caught your son Marcel cheating in his exams" said the teacher.

Look here's your son's paper and here is the one of the pupil next to him, the same answers. Who suceeded Napoleon? … Louis XVIII.

"That's not proof" the father retorted, that answer is correct, they both have it right".

"Ah yes" said the teacher, "but what about the next question?"

"Where was Napoleon exiled to?" Both have replied "The Island of Saint Louis".

"Well yes" said the father "but both of them can get a question wrong. It does happen you know"

"Well, what about this then" said the teacher. "Give me the date of Napoleon's death?"

The other lad had put, "I don't know, and your son, do you know what he put?"

"No" said the father.

"Me neither!"

* * *

On leaving the chateau we stopped in the first village we came to, and went to see if we could leave our questionnaire.

The village bar had only one customer – Monsieur Sevellec. He said he would think about our request and write to us.

After some weeks we received this reply:

"Now I won't tell you a recipe for I am sure you will find many here in France, but instead I will tell you of an old 'cure' handed down to me from my father and from his mother before him.

It is a cure for back pains and arthritis, an old country cure.

If you suffer from such problems, and have been in great pain, you may well be prepared to try anything.

In that case try this as an example.

I met a man who was unable to move for a large portion of his life.

After sitting down at the table, he would often have to slowly slide down off the chair down to the floor, such was his pain.

He then pulled himself slowly up to stand, using the wall as a support.

Now, by using this remedy, he no longer has pain, and is perfectly mobile.

however, you may feel it a strange method of curing back problems, that is why I am taking so long to divulge my secret.

You may not believe, or wish to believe ….the cure is the humble potato!

Not to eat, but to cover the painful area with it. This is what you can do.

Peel a large potato (which has been kept cold in the fridge). Slice it very thinly so you can almost see through the slices, cover the painful area well, overlapping the potatoes.

Keep these slices pressed to the affected area by a bandage, day and night.

Keep the slices in the fridge and change them every day. You must continue this processs for say 3 days more if necessary until you find the pain has gone out of the body.

This can be used for arthritis and rheumatism or on any part of the body. For example wrap the potato slices frequently – you will see the slices go black, but … persevere.

The man I told you about cut to shape, and wore a pair of his wife's tights to keep the potatoes firmly to his lower back, as I say night and day.

Keep them pressed in place – no laughing.

Good health to all

CHAPTER THIRTEEN

Lassale and Co.

There is, alongside the Canal du Midi a tarmacadam path it's very popular for walking the dog, cycling and 'les joggings'.

The canal is lined with old mottled shades of green plane trees which protect from the sun.

It is therefore an ideal place if you are a Dog Food Manufacturer to advertise an event you were sponsoring.

We translated and read the posters which had been stapled to each of the plane trees which lined this popular local section of the canal.

Dimanche 26 September
Come and run with you dog
3 Categories, Cross-vineyard/cyclist and dog/dog chariots'
The events are open to Men and Women,
Juniors 15-18 and Children under 15.

A public address system would be provided courtesy of Lassale & Co.
'Cups' for each event will be awarded to the winners

Each entrant is guaranteed a large free bag of dog biscuits on completing his or her particular course.

Well we couldn't miss this. The events were to be held on a former vineyard, a grande terrain behind the E.Leclerc Supermarche.

GIL'GUY
LA PASSION ET LA FORME

DIMANCHE 26 SEPTEMBRE

VENEZ COURIR avec VOTRE CHIEN

CROSS CANIN DES VENDANGES

DOMAINE DE BASTIT
ZAC MONTIMARAN   SORTIE AUTOROUTE
BEZIERS EST

CATEGORIE **CROSS**   OUVERTE A TOUS
-HOMMES, FEMMES, ENFANTS (- de 15 ANS)
SENIORS, JUNIORS (- de 18 ans)
CATEGORIE **VELO et KART**
RESERVEES LICENCIES

RENSEIGNEMENTS et INSCRIPTIONS
67 35 16 32
ou GALERIE GEANT CASINO
du 17 au 25 09

LASSALE S.A. 25 ANS D'EXPERIENCE DE L'ALIMENTATION ANIMALE

The vines had recently been grubbed-up in an effort to stem the flow of the EU wine lake. In the centre of the vineyard a stage had been set up with an announcer, an adjudicator and a public address system.

All in operation courtesy of Lassale & Co.

On the morning of the event a track had been cleared which zig'zagged around the vineyard. Movable barriers were in place which could be adjusted from track to trace to direct the contestants into ½ km, 1km. And 3km. sections.

Close on 500 people were there and both starting and finishing posts were alongside the stage.

The contestants for the first race were called for on the public address system:

Ladies with dogs on Lead – one kilometre

Various shapes and sizes and breed of dog were brought forth from the crowd by their slim track-suited lady owners.

At the starting line introductions were made to their fellows in the usual canine time-honoured way- a touch of noses and a sniff of the bottom. A snooty look of total indifference to some inferior breed, a growl and a bark by such inferior smaller breed, struggling as if to say "if only I wasn't held back by this lead". A circling, a recircling and disorder.

The Starting official wisely blew his whistle and they were off, around the track they ran, owners pulling dogs, some dogs pulling owners, dogs bumping into other dogs, tripping along and being tripped. One young boxer slipped his lead and ran off into the vineyard, a red setter stopped and cocked a leg.

Some mistresses, obviously very keen for their free bag of biscuits ran full spurt the poor dog being pulled half-way off the ground around the track, all this to cries of support from husbands, from children and from other dogs courtesy of Lassale & Co.

The Men's 3km and Children's ½km events followed a similar pattern.

We were waiting to see just what 'cycles pulled by dogs' could be and it was just that.

Specially created and built, 2 wheeled cycles with a long rope attached to the front – again 2 dogs, (being either Alsatians or Huskies) were attached by cords to the main 'pulling rope'.

There were no pedals and so each contestant had to be pulled sitting astride the bike, he was allowed to push the ground with his feet, or even run alongside the bike.

We were expecting something that was possibly unkind to the dogs, but no, they had done it all before and decided they loved it! and showed it. They couldn't wait.

The whistle blew and off they raced, pulling the bike, with the rider steering and following to some extent the track.

They thoroughly enjoyed it and were rewarded at the end by a cuddle from each one of their human family.

Large bowls of water (courtesy of Lassale & Co) were available, for it was a hot day.

Finally we had the Dog and Bitch Chariot Race. The 'chariots' were bicycle frames adapted into three wheeled vehicles where the rider was positioned on a platform off the ground, and the dogs did all the pulling.

Once again they were straining to get started. Each team had to be held back at the starting line they were so keen to be off.

Most teams were Huskies, blue eyed and quite wolf like and if you looked at him he would return that look with a long stare.

The largest team consisted of three Huskies, an Alsatian and a pit-bull terrier. This team with the red faced owner on high shouting encouragement to his dogs was going so fast that the first corner that his Chariot did an overshoot off the track and ran up and over a banking and plunged at high speed into the 'E.Leclerc' Supermarket car-park! scattering terrified Sunday shoppers all around and all courtesy of Lassale & Co.

Cartoon by Peter Bickerdike

CHAPTER FOURTEEN

A more minor road now, direction 'Labastide-en-Val, a pleasant quiet road. We meanered along in the afternoon sunshine, a sea of vines covered the countryside from horizon to horizon.

We crossed the bridge to enter the village and there, on our left, was an idyllic cottage straight off the cover of a chocolate box, resplendent with a newly mown lawn down to a stream, an immaculately neat vegetable garden, a rotating sprinkler splashing the lush green vegetables.

A gem of a cottage with a dusty pink tiled roof, and alongside one wall stacks of gnarled old vine wood.

The piled branches are called sarments and they are selected being ideal for cooking barbeques.

All looking so peaceful, we decided we'd spend the rest of our lives there – we'd live a life of peace and contentment, a little piece of heaven had fallen to earth. Thank You.

We drove on into the village, dare I spoil it by mentioning it's full of old houses, just ripe for conversion to holiday homes?

A stream ran through the whole length of the village which was spanned by many little stone bridges full of geraniums which trailed along the bridge parapets.

Stone archways crossed the streets and everywhere one looked was cared for, and loved.

Peaceful yes but there was still a strange feeling of sadness everywhere.

Up the village street noisy old taps pounded water continuously into stone troughs.

There was no-one about. We went to explore the Church. We opened the heavy church door and stepped inside.

A commemerative plaque to the 'First World War Dead', shows four of the Bedos family losing their lives.

Marius Bedos – 23.04.84 to 24.09.1914
Gaston Bedos – 15.07.92 to 13.11.1914
Ernest Bados – 22.09.83 to 24.05.1915
Isidore Bedos – 28.05.95 to 09.06.1915

It is impossible to imagine the despair of the Bedos family in this village as news reached them of each boy losing his life

Marius aged 30, killed 24th September, 1914.

Gaston, aged 22, killed just 7 weeks later.

Ernest aged 32, killed 6 months after.

Isidore, aged only 20, 16 days later.

What sadness there must have been in Labastide-en-Val, within that 10 month period.

The village priest found us in his church and took us on a walking tour of his village.

He was very pleased to have English visitors as he was learning English and he wanted to know more about our 'quest' – we explained. He loved the idea and asked if he could join in?

He asked us to wait for a short while and left us, to return, after 10 minutes or so having copied a couple of recipes his housekeeper frequently made for him, and which were, he confirmed, by kissing the two papers, his favourites.

He would be back in a minute he said as he wanted to give us a joke as well.

OYSTER SOUP

　1 quart white stock
　1 ½ dozen oysters
　1 pint of milk
　½ pint cream
　1oz butter
　1oz flour
　a blade of mace
　a strip of lemon peel
　a dust of cayonne pepper

Put the stock on to boil, put the milk into a saucepan with the maze, pepper and lemon peel, (very thinly pared) and bring to the boil.

Draw to one side and let it infuse for about 15 minutes.

Beard the oysters and wash out any grit in their own liquor. Put the beards in the stock to boil. When the stock boils, strain it, and put in on the reboil

Then add the milk which must be strained first.

Rub the flour well into the butter and add this to the soup.

Stir until it thicken, but do not let it boil.

Lastly add the cream. The oysters are added to the soup just before serving.

If the oysters are large they can be cut into two, or even three pieces.

CONFIT D'OIE

　Take:-
　1 goose
　100g (4oz) sea salt
　pork fat or beef dripping

Cut the goose into joints and remove all the fat from inside the goose.

Rub all the joints over with salt, place in an earthenware dish and leave for 5-6 days if it is freshly killed farm goose, or 2-3 days if it is shop bought goose.

Melt the goose fat down, you should have enough to completely cover the goose when it is cooking. If there is insufficient you will have to add a little pork fat or beef dripping.

At the end of the salting time, wash the goose and place in an earthenware or ovenproof dish.

Cover with the fat and cook in a moderate oven – 180c or 350f or gas mark 4, for 2-3 hours or until the goose is quite tender.

Pack the goose into jars or other suitable containers, allow the fat to cool a little then strain over the goose so that it is completely covered.

Cover the jar with paper or foil and use as required.

A Joke

A French village Priest, who was learning English, went into a pet shop and asked if they had a parrot that spoke English.

The shopkeeper said he only had one parrot and that it was bi-lingual.

The parrot was brought forth on it's perch, from the back room, for the customer to examine. Now just why does that parrot have a piece of string attached to each of it's legs" enquired the customer.

The shopkeeper explained, "Well if you pull on the left leg, he speaks English, and if you pull on his right, he speaks French".

"Incredible" said the customer, "but what if you pull on them both?"

"I fall off this b……. perch" said the parrot.

CHAPTER FIFTEEN

Next village outing we found a roadside carpenter's workshop. We peered in through all the dust and entered. I could just make out a figure next to the electrical saw which was whining to a halt at the far end of the workshop. The whole workshop was covered in sawdust particularly the carpenter himself.

I explained our reason for visiting. I apologised for disturbing him and asked if he would be so kind as to help with a regional recipe for our book?

"With pleasure" he said and took the 'questionaire' which he read slowly and carefully, then he folded it slowly and carefully and placed it in his trouser pocket.

He patted the pocket twice and said "pas de probleme Monsieur'!"

It was some two weeks later that the following recipe (and jokes) were left in our post-box.

THE CARPENTER

SARDINES AUX EPINARDS

(SARDINES WITH SPINACH)

Take:
500(1lb) fresh sardines
salt and pepper
1 kg (2 lb) fresh spinach or 500g (1lb) frozen spinach defrosted.
4 tablespoon of olive oil
1 large onion finely chopped
2 cloves of garlic crushed.
2 tablespoons of fresh white breadcrumbs.

Cut the heads off the sardines.

Clean them and season with salt and pepper.

Wash the spinach then cook in 2 tablespoons of salted water until tender.

Drain thoroughly and chop finely.

Heat 2 tablespoons of the oil in a pan and fry the onion gently for about 5 mins.

Add the spinach, garlic and seasoning and mix well.

Turn into the bottom of a lightly greased ovenproof dish place the sardines on top sprinkle with breadcrumbs, then with the remaining olive oil.

Bake in a moderately hot oven 190 degrees C, 375 degrees F, Gas mark 5 for 20 minutes

Serves 4-6 as an hors d'oeuvre or 2-3 as a main course.

His Joke

Two Military career men were swapping memories of their times in the Army

"Why did you join?" asked one "Well because I like fighting and I'm bachelor and you?"

"Me? well, because I'm married and I like peace."

Michel, the butcher, saw his normally able-bodied, friend coming down street sitting in a wheelchair,

"What on earth has happened?" asked Michel

"Ssh say nothing, I've made out I've had an accident on my tractor, so I can claim on my insurance."

"But you're mad" said Michel "You'll have to spend the rest of your days in that wheel chair."

"Not likely" said his friend, "once they've paid up, I'm off on a pilgrimage to LOURDES."

CHAPTER SIXTEEN

The open-air theatre in Valras Plage is situated on the sea front alongside the estuary of the river Orb. Each night, during the summer months, the town provides free entertainment at the Theatre for all the visitors – actually paid for by a 'resort-tax', of one franc per person per day collected through the hotel bill, campsite charge or rental for holiday flats.

These francs are then paid over to the Marie, (Town Hall) who design a full entertainment programme throughout the holiday season. Some shows are very professional others not so, but it's all good fun and everyone enjoys themselves.

Last night was 'Chansons Francaises' at 21.30hrs, a lady singer sang her way through French songs, Ancient et Moderne.

The only problem was the 'competition' she had for attention – on the market place, alongside the Theatre de la Mer, was a large paved area, reserved for the Monday and Friday morning's open-air markets: also dances and wine fetes, a very large crane had been erected for 'saute-elastique' or bungee jumping as it is called.

Jumpers were being hoisted up to the top of the crane on a small platform attached to a cable, with an 'operative' going up with them. His job was to give moral support' along with instructions on the correct method of stepping out onto the 'take off' platform and on how to 'jump' safely.

The pair of them went up in the air comanding every ones attention.

I'm not sure of the actual height of this crane but it looked a very long way up and was higher than the Residence du Port apartment building nearby and that I counted, as having 5 stories!

At the bottom of the crane, an area was set aside, surrounded by barriers for our intrepid 'jumpers' to be kitted- up in ancle straps and a safety strap, fitted around the waist, just in case.

They were then weighed in on a pair of bathroom scales.

A large crowd now surrounded the barriers – the area being illuminated with spotlights and camera flashbulbs, and music is playing.

One of five elastic cables is selected according to the jumpers weight, one end attached to a hook on the jumping platform and the other strapped to the ankles and waist of the participant.

Cost? … 250 francs per jump!!! … approximately (£27.00)

They don't seem short of customers either, all evening a continuous queue of brave young things had been leaping off the high platform. I think the style they adopt in diving-board terms is called a 'swallow dive'. They plunge ¾ of the way down before being jerked up again as the elastic reaches its full length, then they bob up and down before being lowered back to terre firma. The 'demonstrator' who did a few guest appearances', when it as necessary to attract more customers, actually got so close to the ground he picked up a red demonstration hankerchief from a small coffee table!

The area was busy with people bungee watching, or going to and from the Theatre, there is no need to book a seat at the theatre, it's free and open-air, just come and go as you please, people arrive, sit down for 5 minutes and stroll off again. Children play in the aisles and a peanut vendor, dressed in Mexican hat, and what lookks like silk pyjamas passes along each row, torch in hand, handing out 'free samples of his sugar-coated peanuts'

The bags are 10 francs a time, should you wish to buy one. It it is generally believed that he is a very wealthy man having a large villa in nearby Beziers.

The whole evening looks totally disorganised and probably is, but it's all very relaxed and good humoured.

If the sound man doesn't think the microphone is too clear he'll bob down and creep along the front of the stage during an act and change it, often when a performer is in mid-song. The French seem to take this for granted, he is, after all an 'expert' and therefore to be respected.

At an earlier show in the week, we saw another sound man, with his consol at the back of the theatre, (cables everywhere by the way) spend almost the whole evening striding down the right-hand aisle, cocking an ear to the speakers there, striding back to adjust his master control knobs, then down the left hand aisle, cocking an ear to the left hand speakers, then back to the consol until he was satisfied, this took up most of the performance, his 'performance' was more compulsive viewing than that of those performing on the stage.

Our lady singer, of the night in question, was in fact very good and had done excellent Edith Piaff imitations. At the moment she was in mighty voice, rendering and, it's in all singer's repetoires, 'Comme d'Habitude', but she was singing it in English which is considered more 'chic'.

"And now the end is near, and so I face the final curtain",

Her seated audience in the open-air Theatre turned their heads in turn to look up at the illuminated jump platform.

When it reached the top of the crane further spotlights lit the platform. The audience would watch as the jumpers took the plunge.

"I've lived a life that's full, I've travelled each and every highway",

A young girl aged about 14, reached the top, who must have spent most of her holiday money on this one moment of glory. Clearly she was very nervous. she stepped out onto the swaying take-off platform, and then rushed back into the arms of the operator. He was trying to persuade her to jump.

One by one the Theatre audience turned to look behind, and up at the girl. She had been there a full 5 minutes, hesitating, then stepping out and back again.

The crowd at the base of the crane, started counting dix … neuf … huit … sept:

"Yes, there were times, I'm sure you knew"

"When I bit off more than I could chew"

Further members of the audience in the Theatre joined in, Six, Cinq, Quatre.

The singer on the stage motioned to the sound man, who gradually lowered the volume, and then stopped the sound on her backing tape, (no orchestra) she stopped singing to see for herself what would happen.

Trois, Deux, Une, the girl stepped out onto the spot-lit platform, but straight back again!

Someone unkindly (I wonder how courageous they would have been?) started a slow hand clap. By this time she must have been up there 10 minutes, out and back again. It was possible that the whole town was watching from the audience in the Theatre de la Mer, the children at the fun-fair, to the crowd at the base of the crane: those in the pavement cafes and those who paused their strolling along the sea-front promenade.

All were to staring at this little girl a lone frightened figure, spotlighted against the night sky.

Once again again she stepped out onto the high platform! and the crowd, as one, started … DIX … NEUF … HUIT …it is of course very easy to be brave in these circumstances, when you are at ground level, not swaying up there high above the town, she must have had a magnificient view, if she was looking at it in those terms, the fairground lights, lights of Cap d'Agde in the distance, some 20 kilometres along the coast, the sweep of the beaches up to the river Orb, and looking down over the sparkling town of Valras Plage and all along the promenade!

… TROIS … DEUX … UNE

SHE JUMPED!

It was as if the whole town applauded!!!

There was cheering everywhere, while she bobbed up and down. At a signal from the singer – the tape started up again, the Theatre audience turned their heads back towards the stage and the singer on the Theatre stage continued to the end of her song.

"the record shows, I took the blows,

and I did it

My Way."

Vin conseillé :   Béziers.
un côté de
Provence, blanc   **Bouillabaisse** (plat à base de
ou rosé   ~~vin~~   poissons de
     de l'Hérault   Méditerranée)
pour 4 personnes

- 1 kg. poissons à chair ferme
  (rascasse + baudroie ou lotte de mer
  grondin + congre)
- 1 kg poissons à chair tendre (Saint-Pierre +
  merlan)
- ½ litre de vin blanc
- 3 tomates bien mûres
- 2 oignons, 1 gros poireau   Ecaillez scale
- 1 brin de céleri   videz-gut
- 6 gousses d'ail
- thym + laurier
- 1 litre huile olive -
- ½ à café de safran - sel - poivre.

Mettre de l'huile dans une cocotte ou faitout, faire revenir les légumes coupés en petits morceaux, ajouter l'ail écrasée au presse-ail, et le safran - salez, poivrez et laissez cuire sur feu moyen 5 minutes.

Cuisson des poissons : Posez sur ces légumes les poissons nettoyés et vidés à chair ferme - ajoutez de l'eau bouillante salée et poivrée pour recouvrir les poissons, laissez cuire pendant 7 minutes et à découvert. puis ajoutez les poissons à chair tendre laissez cuire 8 minutes et à découvert et ajouter le vin blanc et laisser cuire 10 minutes - ajoutez de la crème fraîche (si cela vous plaît) Préparez des croûtons de pain (faire griller des petits morceaux de pain et ~~frottez les~~ avec de l'ail - Servir très chaud accompagné
Bon Appétit   de croûtons et pommes vapeur

CHAPTER SEVENTEEN

Here are some recipes from the villages of Murviel les Beziers and surrounding area.

BOUILLABAISSE

3 pounds firm fleshed fish (equal parts mackerel, bass or haddock)
3 pounds tender flesh fish (equal parts sole, cod, flounder, whiting or red snapper)
¾ cup olive oil
3 cups chopped onions (3 large)
3 cups finely cut leeks (or 2 more cups onions)
4 cloves garlic mashed
2 cups dry white wine
2 pounds fresh tomatoes, peeled and chopped or a can tomatoes coursley chopped
1 bottle (8oz) clam juice
½ teaspoon dried orange peel (optional)
1 tsp. Thyme
1 tsp. Saffron crumbled
1 tsp fennel seeds crushed
2 bay leaves
1 tsp. Salt
½ tsp. Pepper
¼ chopped parsley – stems reserved
2 or 3 live lobsters (1 pound)
1 pound fresh shrimps
12 small clams well scrubbbed (optional)
French breadcrumbs

Preparation

Cut fish into 2-inch pieces, bone an'all.

Keep firm and tender fleshed fish seperate, they will be added to the kettle at different times.

Heat oil in large stainless steel or enamelled kettle over medium heat . Add onions and leeks. Cook 5 minutes stirring often add garlic, cook one minute.

Add wine, tomatoes, clam juice and orange peel , herbs, seasonings and parsley stems. Bring to boiling. Cook 5 minutes.

Cut live lobsters into 2-inch pieces shells an' all. Place in kettle.

Top with firm fleshed fish. Bring to boil. Cook 10 minutes or until the clams open.

Remove fish and shellfish to warm serving dish.

Discard bay leaves and parsley stems.

Bring liquid to boil . Pour over fish.

Sprinkle with fresh chopped parsley.

Serve with bread. Makes 12 servings.

FISH SOUP

2lb of Fish (see below)
½ pint shrimps 2 oz butter
1 pint milk
2oz flour
3 pints water
2 carrots
1 Leek
½ stick celery
A bunch of herbs (Bayleaf, Thyme and Parsley)
a blade of mace
pepper and salt

Any white fish answers for this soup such as Haddock, Whiting or Plaice, Cod etc.

Take 2 pounds in all but half of this may be trimmings.

Wash them well and cut them into small pieces and chop the bones.

Put all into a sauce pan with three pints of cold water.

Add the vegetables which must be washed well and thinly sliced.

Pick out the shrimps, tie the shells in a piece of muslin and put them into the soup, the shrimps are kept for garnishing '

Also put in the herbs and mace but not the chopped parsley.

Bring to the boil and skim well.

Add the seasoning and boil for two hours, until the vegetables are quite tender.

Strain the soup through a fine sieve into a basin.

Remove the two muslim bags containing the herbs and shrimp shells.

With a wooden spoon rub as much of the fish and vegetables as possibly through the sieve but be careful that no bones go through.

Melt the butter in a saucepan, mix in the flour then gradualy stir in the milk.

Stir all the time until it boils.

Rinse out the soup saucepan, return the soup to it and add the thickened milk.

Stirring until it almost boils.

Just before serving add the finely chopped parsley and the pickled shrimps.

If required add a little more seasoning.

CHAPTER EIGHTEEN

Not of this region however

This villager says "I am not of this region so neither is my recipe. It is not for you – but you will find it equal to any other you may collect hereabouts."

ENCHAUD PERIGOURDIN FROID

48 hours before:	15 minutes preparation
Night before:	3 ½ hours cooking
Days itself:	15 minutes preparation, 50 minutes cooking

For eight people

1.8 kg filet of pork
2 kg potatoes
1 large endive
1 bunch of parsley
5 cloves of garlic
120ml of beef stock (made from concentrate)
5 soupspoons of lard
oil, wine, vinegar
salt and pepper
A large pot with lid

2 days before:

Buy meat – lay meat out on a work surface. Peel 4 cloves of garlic, crush them and place all over meat. Pepper generously – add salt.

Roll up the meat and tie with string. Refrigerate for a day.

Day before:

Heat three spoonfulls of lard in a pan over a gentle heat, bown meat for around 20 minutes. Heat oven No. 5 170C.

Put meat in the pot. Make sauce with remaining juices. Add cooking juices and dab meat with rest of lard. Cook for three hours. After an hour turn the heat down to gas mark 4, 150C.

When cooked take out of oven but don't lift lid. Leave to cool for a few hours and then refrigerate.

The day itself:

1 hour before the meal, peel potatoes and slice. Open the pot and remove two or three spoonful's of congealed fat around the meat. Cover up and refrigerate again.

Heat the spoonful's of fat in a frying pan and once hot add potatoes and brown over a fairly high heat, turning frequently with a wooden spatula.

Peel and crush the fifth clove of garlic, chop parsley and mix together – as soon as the potatoes begin to brown, sprinkle this mixture over them. Cover and lower the heat. Cook over a gentle heat for 40 minutes, turning the potatoes every 10 minutes.

Before the potatoes are cooked, wash and dry chicory. Prepare the vinaigrette.

Take the pork out of the pot, take of all the fat – keeping it for future use. Take off string – cut the meat into fairly thin slices and place on a large platter.

Put potatoes around meat. Serve separately.

Recommended wine:

Stay in my region with a red Cotes be Bergerac, preferably a young one with character, although not too full-bodied, or a rustic red whose light acidity will balance well the taste of the cold pork fat.

CHAPTER NINETEEN

Driving habits

French driving habits

The number of times I've seen a car in the mirror gradually getting closer and closer, only for him to get close enough to see the car he has in front has a 'GB sticker '. Well that's it, like a red rag to a bull and with great panache, he closes to within inches of the back bumper then, with inscrutable nerve and accelerating noisily like mad, he closely skirts past … Agincourt! and Joan of Ark avenged!

Then you find, just as he's got in front, that the turn-off he wants is immediately to the right! So you have to brake sharply to avoid running into the back of him, as he roars off into the countryside.

This manoeuvre he can perform with even more daringly if he has a lady passenger with him.

And parking, well parking is just about anywhere, on traffic islands, blocking side streets, 'double' parking is quite normal, anything goes. However, to be fair if you arrive at a holdup, – the driver, being in say a shop or in a bar and blocking the road then one has only to give the horn a toot, for the owner to emerge smiling, from a smoke filled cafe, leaving his morning pastis for the moment, and with an apologetic smile and a wave of the hand, he will move his car further onto the pavement, so you can get by.

And what about the Gendarmes?

Well here's a 'for instance', we stopped at a roadside 'Relais Routier' Restaurant for lunch the other day. Outside in the car park were two large police motorcycles, inside were two policemen at the bar, guns – in holsters, beers in hand, after two beers each, they sat down for lunch, in the crowded restaurant, all tables taken, lorry drivers all. And our two policemen. After a couple of bottles of wine per table, and a good lunch, the jovial company left to join the hustle and bustle of life on French roads.

We stayed rooted to the spot in the emptied restaurant, calculating how long it would be for everyone to sober up!

And here's another 'for instance' whilst driving in the perfectly correct British manner on the main road, through this village of Murviel-les-Beziers, a driver, (who was on his own) pulled out of a side street immediately in front of us! There was a clear white line across the road to indicate that he should 'stop' for the main road, but no – he didn't even glance in our direction!

Exasperated and braking hard to avoid a collision- with natural Anglo Saxon self-control, I refrained from giving him a blasting on my horn.

I then saw the sign on top of his car 'AUTO-ECOLE!! – yes, yer actual driving instructor!

So what chance is there?

CHAPTER TWENTY

Double Decker

If you are approaching Narbonne, on the Route National from Perpignan, you will see on entering the industrial zone south of the city in a scrapyard, alongside the road and placed high on the top of a pile of scrap cars and lorrries and standing proudly – a red British double decker bus with open platform . It has obviously been there for years and is positioned in such a way as to be seen from a distance and so has become a local 'land mark'. So to advertise the scrap yard.

Seeing this for the first time, double deckers are largely unknown in France, was quite a surprise.

A Tip – In Narbonne near this bus is a "Boulangerie" Chez Constantin.

We told the Baker of our quest and his response? Do tell your clients to visit me if they are in the area and sample the taste of my most delicious bread.

This recipe was prepared for us by Constantin himself.

CHEZ CONSTANTIN

SNAILS – escargots. Only certain VARIETIES OF SNAILS ARE EDIBLE so if you are preparing the dish yourself make sure you use the right version!

Boil the snails for an hour, add salt, bay leaf and thyme.

Drain the escargots.

Separately – brown cubes of ham with finely chopped parsley and nuts, add tomatoe puree.

Mix well and leave to cook for around an hour.

Add ingredients all together.

At the end add garlic and mayonnaise.

All this should be accompanied by a "Fitou" and a good French loaf from "Chez Constantin".

BRIOCHE

Ingredients
4 cups of flour, 1 cup of butter
¾ cake yeast
a pinch of salt
1 tablespoon sugar
8 eggs

Take about ¼ cup of the flour and mix it with the yeast and a little warm milk and put the resulting dough in a warm place to prove. Sift the rest of the flour and place in a bowl.

Make a 'well' and place 6 of the eggs, the sugar, the salt and make all into a fairly stiff dough.

Work in the remainer of the eggs and then mix in the butter. Add the dough and set aside to prove – keep in a cold place covered cloth.

You can keep it like this for 8 or 9 hours but it is best to leave it overnight. In the morning add a little warm milk- as much as is needed and knit until it is smooth and silky.

Leave it to rise again.

When risen, place in small brioche moulds which can be bought at any good kitchen equipment shop. The mould should be about 2 1/2 inches deep.

Cut from your dough small pieces and make them in round balls.

Take much smaller pieces and make them into smaller balls.

Then make a 'hole' in each of the larger balls and place the smaller on top.

They should look like little cottage loafs.

Leave them to rest for about half an hour and then wash over with the yoke of an egg.

If you put a little sugar in the yolk of the egg it will make the cooked "Brioche" a little browner.

Bake in a 350 degree oven for about 30 minutes.

and Constantin's joke?

A man went into a bookshop and said to the lady at the counter:

"Bonjour Madame I'm looking for a book by Pierre Dupont. It's called 'Man the Stronger Sex'"

"Ah" she said, "You want 'Fiction' at the other end of the shop"

Same bookshop, "Do you have a copy of 'How to Commit Suicide' I can't see it on the shelves?"

"No, that's because they never bring 'em back!"

CHAPTER TWENTY ONE

A Fricassee

From Rennes-les-bains – the tabac/ journal shop

The fricassee is a dish – base of porc, which is part of the cultural heritage of our region. It is accompanied with a white haricot beans, cooked in goose fat.

FRICASSEE

> Take 1 kilo of meat (neck or boned shoulder) of pork, a little of the pig's heart, 3 medium sized onions some cloves of garlic, herbs, a little tomato paste – ½ glass of cognac.
> (no specific quantities given I'm afraid)

Cut pork into small pieces, the heart finely chopped, and brown with sliced onions and chopped garlic. Throw in half a glass of cognac and flambe – stir well so all the pieces of meat absorb the cognac. Mix well and add tomato paste, salt, peper and herbs – cover with a mix of hot water and a soup spoon of vinegar.

When meat is cooked, (slowly for about three hours in a cocotte (casserole dish), prepare a little flour in cold water, stir and place in the fricassee to thicken.

Add bouquet garni or more herbs and serve.

And this from the same village – the Gendarmerie

1/ Rennes-les-Bains

La Fricassée est un plat à base de porc et qui fait partie de l'héritage culturel de notre région. Elle s'accompagne de haricots blancs cuisinés à la graisse d'oie.

Fricassée. 1 kilogramme d'Echine de porc un peu de coeur de filet 3 oignons moyens, quelques grains d'ail, des aromates, un peu de coulis de tomate.

Faire dorer le porc coupé en petits morceaux avec oignons et ail. Ajouter une demi tasse de cognac et flamber, en remuant bien pour que tous les morceaux soient imbibés. puis ajouter le coulis de tomate sel et poivre aromates. couvrir avec de l'eau chaude et une cuillerée à soupe de vinaigre. Quand la viande est cuite. Préparer un peu de farine dans de l'eau froide remuer, et mettre dans la sauce pour la lier. enlever le bouquet garni ou les aromates et servez.

2/ Légende sur le tresor de Rennes le château bien connu dans la région.

3 Paysages très divers aux alentours de Rennes les Bains forêts, sources, botanique, et geologie. Vestiges Gallo Romains.

MOULES A L'OSEILLE

(MUSSELS WITH SORREL)

Take 3 quarts of cleaned mussels
1 tablespoon olive oil
3 large glasses dry white wine
2 tablespoons chopped parsley
3 cloves garlic
2oz mild gammon
Serves 4 to 6

Put the mussels to open in a wide pan with white wine and cook rapidly.

Remove as soon as they are open and shell them.

Dice the gammon finely as possible and chop the garlic.

Heat the oil in a pan and sauté the mussels, together with the gammon, garlic, parsley for 3 or 4 minutes.

Serve on a bed of 'fondu d' oseille' (sorrel leaves) with triangles of fried bread arranged around the dish.

And from the Insurance Agency

BOUILLABAISSE

2 kg of fish with firm hard flesh, eg. Scorpion fish, burbot &
red gurnard, and conger
1½ kg. Of white fish eg. John Dory + whiting
3 ripe tomatoes
2 onions
1 large leek
1 small stick of celery
6 gloves of garlic
1 bouguet garni
a few pieces of fennel
1 stale baguette
stale breadcrumbs

1 chilli pepper
milk, salt and pepper
¼ litre of olive oil
½ tsp of saffron
a large stewpot

Preparation

Put a large handful of breadcrumbs in some milk. De-scale, gut and wash fish.

Cut the large ones into large pieces, leave the small ones whole.

Cut the baguette into slices of about 1 cm thickness, toast them and rub garlic on one side (this will use about 2 cloves).

Peel onions, clean leek after cutting green bits off. Wash celery, chop these vegetables, peel tomatoes and remaining clove of garlic.

Heat 200ml of oil in saucepan, cook vegetables for a few minutes, stirring occasionally with a wooden spatula.

Add tomatoes, crush them up, add 2 cloves of crushed garlic, fennel and three pieccess of saffron. Season and cook over a medium heat for around 5 minutes.

Cooking fish

Place the firm fleshed fish on the vegetables. Leave to cook for 5 minutes on a high heat with lid off. Check seasoning and add white fish. Cook for a further 8 minutres, again on high heat and without the lid.

Whilst fish is cooking prepare the 'rouille'. Crush the last 2 cloves of garlic with chilli pepper, slowly add moist breadcrumbs to this mixture. Then add the remaining 50ml of olive oil – bit by bit, blending the oil in all the time.

When the fish are cooked, carefully place them in a large warm serving dish. Strain the stew and use half to cover fish. Keep the liquid and remaining stew in a warm bowl.

Serve very hot, each person takes a couple of croutons and puts some of the rouille in their bowl (be careful as it is very hot/spicy) to which is added the fish stew and liquid.

Recommended wine:-

Cotes de Provence – white rather musky flavour will counter the vigorous bite of the garlic. For the more refined raffiner a 'blanc de cassis' (cherry liquor and white wine).

And from the Estate Agents (two versions)

GARLIC SOUP
(SOUP A L'AIL)

Take 16 cloves of garlic, simmer in a casserole in approximately 2 tablespoons of olive oil.

Add 1½ litres of stock, salt and pepper to taste. Cover gently for 15 minutes. Strain the soup and serve with pieces of toasted bread.

GARLIC SOUP

Serves four people
Take the following ingredients:
6 cloves of garlic
1 soup of goose fat or pork fat
4 eggs
3 pints of water
8 drops of vinegar
1 soup spoon of flour
salt and pepper

In a casserole heat the goose fat and fry very finely chopped garlic until golden. Add the water with one soup spoon of flour, very gradually make sure there are no lumps, allow to boil adding salt and pepper to taste.

Separate the eggs and place whites together in the casserole, stir so the egg whites break into small pieces.

Continue simmering for a further 20 minutes. Take the egg yolks, add the drops of vinegar and a small amount of water (a soup spoon) pour the yolks mixture over the soup.

Take off the heat after 3 minutes only and serve hot.

And the jokes?

From the tabac/ journal

   A little boy asked his teacher at the end of the day.

   "Can you tell me what I have learnt today? – because my daddy asks me that every evening when I get home."

From the gendarmerie

   Two ladies were gossiping in a Salon de The.

   "Do you know that the Baron du Vallon is completely ruined half his friends have turned their backs on him"

   "and the other half?"

   they haven't yet heard he's ruined!"

From the Insurance Agency

A French Bank official said to his work colleague

"My wife has finally found a part time job."

"Oh yes in what sector?"

"Well she 'child-minds' for our cleaning lady!"

From the Estate Agents

A little boy visiting the Zoo for the first time, with his father, enquired

"Papa why do giraffes have such long necks?"

"Well, that's how they have evolved – it's so they can eat the leaves of trees" replied Papa.

"And why then do they have such long legs?" asked the little boy.

"Well," replied Papa. "It's because their necks weren't quite long enough."

From the Tourist Office

"What will you have for breakfast Jean-Piere now you've decided to be a vegetarian?" asked his wife.

"Well I couldn't possibly eat anything that has come from an animal's flesh."

"So, what's it to be?"

"I'll have a boiled egg."

CHAPTER TWENTY TWO

Those dogs again

The French 'adore' their dogs they carry them everywhere like babies cradled in their arms, inside a shopping bag with just a head popping out or sitting upright in baskets in front of their bikes – watching all that is going on.

The latest 'fashion' for dogs is for them to wear a 'cap' or 'casquette pour chien' as it's called with a matching cravatte (69francs and 25 francs respectively from the local market).

The dog is without doubt a member of the family, we saw a restaurant table the other evening , set for six. Mum and Dad 3 children and the dog <u>sat</u> with his cap on! on a chair at the table with them so they could feed him titbits, we didn't stop to see what his table manners were like!

On another occasion we saw a very sophisticated lady at a table in a pavement cafe with a poodle, eating ice cream, dog on her knee a spoonful for her, one for the dog, one for her etc. and the same spoon, that's going a bit too far for us!

A small survey of dog food tin labels in the local supermarket reads like the menu of some gourmet restaurant:

Pate morceaux viandes aux legumes

Patee aux volaille

Plat cuisine au Boeuf et petites legumes

Bouchees au boeuf aux carottes et au riz

Boulettes a la volaille

Boulettes aux viandes

'bon appetit'!

At the airport in Montpellier staff at the local Chamber of Commerce kiosk (which is in the airport arrival lounge to welcome any business men and women and promote products of the region) a number of the staff there were very interested in our requests in our Questionnaires! They offered to help with their own favourites – here they are.

BAY LEAF POTATOES
(FROM THE STAFF AT MONTPELLIER AIRPORT)

Rrequired number of Potatoes
fresh Bay Leaf
garlic
crème fraiche
butter
saffron
salt and pepper
Cook the potatoes for about 20 minutes in a steamer
crush garlic

Heat oven.

Put each potato in a piece of aluminium foil – cut open the potatoes and slip in a bayleaf and some garlic into each, add salt and pepper.

Close each parcel and cook in oven for about 30 minutes.

Put butter, crème fraiche and a bit of water in a saucepan. Bring to the boil add salt and pepper and saffron.

Serve potatoes with sauce.

Inland villages – I recomend tourists to wander around the area, to stop in villages and to look as there are many interesting things one notices things that one misses if one drives straight past, one needs to be curious!

BOURRIDE OF EEL

The Bouride (stew) is a typical Mediterranean dish. It is also a firm favourite of the fishing community in Languedoc Roussillon.

The eel is highly prized for the quality of it's very delicate meat. This bourride can also be made using turbot

Recipe for 6 people
Preparation time 45 minutes
Cooking time 20 minutes

Ingredients
200gms of rancid lard
3 cloves of garlic
3 eggs
3 cayonne peppers (dried chilli peppers?)
a few grains of aniseed
Toasted breadcrumbs
½ litre of olive oil
600gms of eel
400grm of potatoes
2 thin slices of dried ham
Salt and pepper

Make a pomade with the fat(lard) and dried ham.

Melt this mixture in a casserole dish under a medium heat.

Peel and wash potatoes, cut them into slices of about 2/3 centimetres thickness.

Add potatoes to the melted pomade.

Cover with water Add peppers and aniseed.

Scrape the eels with sand to get rid of the glue one finds on the skin.

Remove heads and fillet eels.

Add eels to potatoes and cook for 20 minutes.

Prepare 'aioli' ie put garlic in a bowl, add salt, pepper, 3 egg yolks. Beat into a mayonnaise.

Slice 3 pieces of bread for each person, add garlic to each and toast.

When 20 minutes of cooking is up mix the 'aioli' to the bourride.

Decorate shallow bowls with toasted bread and serve bourride.

NB No mention of the ½ litre of olive oil? Maybe for the toast.

OLLADA

Serves 6 people

Ingredients
7 Leeks ½ carrot
5 turnips
½ tin of haricot beans
1 small cabbage
a large handful of French beans
1kg of potatoes
100g of pearl barley
½ kg. 'Coustellou' (pork ribs)
1 pigs tail
6 Black puddings
600gm sausages
'garu' 2 strips of dried ham
a knob of 'sagi' (lard not too rancid)

Preparation 1 hour (depending on quantity)
Cooking time: 3 – 6 hours

Peel and wash vegetables.

Chop the 'coustellou and **pigs tails**.

Put the garu in cold water and boil until cooked.

Put the vegetables and pieces of coustella in a large casserole dish almost cover with cold water – bring to the boil and simmer for at least two hours.

Add the pearl barley (take care that the pearl barley doestn't stick to the bottom of the dish, continue to cook, add the garu and sagi.

Add sliced potatoes.

When everything has nearly finished cooking, add the haricot beans.

Cook the black puddings – prick them so they don't burst.

Grill the sausages.

To serve:-

Drain the black puddings. Cut the garu and sausages into pieces and place on a warmed plate with gerkings and small pickled onions to garnish.

Serve the vegetables separately in a large bowl.

This 'ollada' is a typical Catalan dish – a unique dish.

To accompany this meal one should have a good green salad with garlic vinaigrette followed by a piece of Roquefort to finish.

WILD BOAR STEW

for 4 people:-

In a little oil, brown the pieces of boar cut from the shoulder or back.

Season.

Add garlic and finely chopped onions, one spoonful of flour and tomato puree.

Steep in ½ litre of Corbier rouge.

Add a touch of water to cover meat.

Check seasonings. Cook for around 2 hours to reduce the sauce.

"Bon Appetit"

"Ollada"   pour au moins 6 personnes

Ingrédient
Légumes : Poireaux   7   Viandes
          Carottes   ½   - Coustellou (plat de côtes de porc) ½ kg
          Navets   5
          Haricots blancs [½ bte au naturel]   queue de porc   1
                          conserve   Boudins noirs   6
          Choux vert   1 petit
          Haricots verts 1 grosse poignée   - saucisse   600 g
          Pommes de terre 1 kg   - "garri" (talons de jambon sec) 2
          Orge perlé   150 g   - une noix de "sagi" (saindoux
                                                                pas trop rance)

Préparation 1 heure (selon quantité)
Cuisson   3 à 6 heures

1. Éplucher et laver les légumes
2. Faire des morceaux avec le "coustellou" et la queue de porc
3. Mettre dans l'eau froide les "garri" et les faire bouillir
   jusqu'à cuisson
4. Mettre les légumes et les morceaux de "coustellou" dans une
   grande cocotte et couvrir largement d'eau froide faire bouillir.
   Cuire au moins 2 heures à petit bouillon

   Ajouter l'orge perlé (faire attention car il a tendance à
   coller au fond de la marmite. Continuer toujours la cuisson.
   Ajouter le "garri" - et le "sagi"

   Mettre les pommes de terre en cubes

   Quand tout est presque cuit - mettre les haricots blancs.

   Faire réchauffer les boudins noirs (piqués pour qu'ils n'éclatent pas)
5. Faire griller la saucisse.

   Au moment de servir : Dresser les boudins égouttés
                le "garri" coupé en morceaux et la saucisse
                dans un plat chaud garni avec des cornichons et
                des petits oignons au vinaigre.
           Les légumes se servent à part dans une soupière.

Cette "ollada" est un plat typique catalan et un plat unique
Il s'accompagne d'une bonne salade verte avec une vinaigrette à l'ail
           Ensuite un morceau de Roquefort termine le repas.

TWENTY THREE

This morning in our little post box on the ground floor arrived a recipe for Frogs Legs! and it came from a town only a short distance away- FRONTIGNAN! – (See first pages of this book)

Although I had asked a number of our 'questionnaire responders' particularly to find a frog's legs menu, none had arrived until <u>now</u> and it will be used to conclude this fun little book.

Thanks for reading it, simply a story of our love for this part of the world its food its wines, its people and some very unusual (to us) recipes, which we hope we have managed to share with you.

Now, to conclude, is the appropriate recipe – it's from a master chef as well!

J.J VALLON lecturer in Cuisine who owns the restaurant at

Le Jas d'Or, 2 Bd. Vistor Hugo 34110 Frontignan

Tel no. 67-43-07-57

(closed Wednesday out of season)

here it is … it is for six people.